EMMANUEL JOSEPH

Green Ventures, Pioneering Sustainability and Ethical Practices in the Global Arena

Copyright © 2025 by Emmanuel Joseph

All rights reserved. No part of this publication may be reproduced, stored or transmitted in any form or by any means, electronic, mechanical, photocopying, recording, scanning, or otherwise without written permission from the publisher. It is illegal to copy this book, post it to a website, or distribute it by any other means without permission.

First edition

This book was professionally typeset on Reedsy.
Find out more at reedsy.com

Contents

1	Chapter 1: The Genesis of Green Ventures	1
2	Chapter 2: The Eco-Economics Paradigm	3
3	Chapter 3: Harnessing Renewable Resources	5
4	Chapter 4: Building a Green Supply Chain	7
5	Chapter 5: Innovating with Green Technology	9
6	Chapter 6: Community Engagement and Corporate Social...	11
7	Chapter 7: Navigating Regulatory Landscapes	13
8	Chapter 8: Ethical Marketing and Consumer Trust	15
9	Chapter 9: Overcoming Industry Resistance	17
10	Chapter 10: The Power of Collaboration	19
11	Chapter 11: Measuring Impact and Sustainability Metrics	21
12	Chapter 12: Navigating Financial Challenges	23
13	Chapter 13: Scaling Sustainable Practices Globally	25
14	Chapter 14: Inspiring the Next Generation	27
15	Chapter 15: The Future of Green Ventures	29

1

Chapter 1: The Genesis of Green Ventures

In the heart of the bustling metropolis, a visionary entrepreneur named Lila Patel found herself disillusioned by the prevailing corporate practices. Lila's passion for sustainability, born from her childhood visits to her grandparents' lush, organic farm, ignited a spark. Her vision was to create a business that not only thrived in the competitive market but also fostered environmental stewardship. Thus, Green Ventures was born, a beacon of hope in the midst of relentless industrialization. The company's inception was marked by a commitment to ethical practices and sustainable growth, setting it apart from its contemporaries.

From its humble beginnings, Green Ventures faced numerous challenges. The initial resistance from investors and stakeholders who were skeptical of the viability of a sustainability-focused business model was daunting. However, Lila's unwavering dedication and strategic vision attracted a small but passionate group of supporters. Together, they embarked on a journey to prove that profitability and sustainability could coexist harmoniously. This chapter delves into the early days of Green Ventures, highlighting the key milestones and turning points that shaped the company's foundation.

As Green Ventures began to gain traction, it became clear that Lila's vision extended beyond mere business success. She envisioned a future where businesses played a pivotal role in addressing global environmental challenges. This chapter explores how Green Ventures embraced innovation and creativity to develop products and services that not only met market demands but also contributed positively to the planet. From eco-friendly packaging to energy-efficient manufacturing processes, Green Ventures set new standards in the industry.

The genesis of Green Ventures was not just about creating a successful business; it was about pioneering a movement. This chapter concludes by reflecting on the broader impact of Green Ventures' early efforts. By challenging conventional business practices and advocating for sustainability, Green Ventures inspired other companies to re-evaluate their own operations. The ripple effect of Green Ventures' pioneering spirit set the stage for a new era of responsible business, laying the groundwork for the company's future growth and influence in the global arena.

2

Chapter 2: The Eco-Economics Paradigm

Green Ventures ventured into uncharted territory by integrating the principles of eco-economics into its business model. By prioritizing sustainability over short-term profits, the company redefined what it meant to be a successful enterprise. This chapter explores the economic theories underpinning Green Ventures' approach, illustrating how ethical practices can indeed coexist with financial viability. It delves into case studies of early successes, shedding light on the path Green Ventures paved for others to follow.

Eco-economics, also known as ecological economics, is an interdisciplinary field that seeks to address the interdependence between human economies and natural ecosystems. Green Ventures recognized that traditional economic models often overlooked the environmental costs of production and consumption. By adopting an eco-economic perspective, the company aimed to balance economic growth with environmental preservation. This chapter examines the key principles of eco-economics and how Green Ventures applied them in its operations.

One of the critical aspects of Green Ventures' eco-economic approach was the implementation of a triple bottom line framework, which evaluates business performance based on three dimensions: people, planet, and profit. This holistic approach allowed Green Ventures to assess the social, environmental, and financial impacts of its activities. This chapter provides detailed examples of how the triple bottom line framework guided decision-making within the company and led to sustainable outcomes.

The success of Green Ventures in adopting an eco-economic paradigm did not go unnoticed. This chapter concludes by discussing the broader implications of Green Ventures' approach for the business community and policymakers. By demonstrating that sustainable business practices can lead to long-term profitability and resilience, Green Ventures set a powerful example for other companies to follow. The chapter also highlights the importance of continued innovation and collaboration in advancing the field of eco-economics and addressing global sustainability challenges.

3

Chapter 3: Harnessing Renewable Resources

G reen Ventures' commitment to renewable resources was a cornerstone of its operations. This chapter delves into the intricate details of how the company transitioned from conventional energy sources to harnessing solar, wind, and hydro power. The journey was fraught with challenges, from initial resistance within the industry to technical hurdles. However, the company's determination and innovative solutions not only overcame these obstacles but also set a precedent for others to emulate.

The transition to renewable energy was driven by Green Ventures' recognition of the environmental and economic benefits of reducing dependence on fossil fuels. This chapter explores the various renewable energy projects undertaken by the company, including the installation of solar panels on manufacturing facilities, the development of wind farms, and the implementation of hydroelectric systems. Each project is examined in detail, highlighting the technical innovations and strategic partnerships that made them successful.

One of the key challenges Green Ventures faced in harnessing renewable resources was the initial capital investment required for infrastructure development. This chapter discusses the financial strategies employed by the company to secure funding for renewable energy projects, including partnerships with green investment funds and government grants. The company's ability to attract investment and demonstrate the economic viability of renewable energy initiatives played a crucial role in overcoming financial barriers.

The chapter concludes by reflecting on the broader impact of Green Ventures' renewable energy initiatives. By demonstrating the feasibility and benefits of renewable energy, Green Ventures inspired other businesses and communities to pursue similar projects. The company's success also contributed to the advancement of renewable energy technologies and the development of supportive policies and regulations. The chapter underscores the importance of continued investment in renewable energy as a critical component of global sustainability efforts.

4

Chapter 4: Building a Green Supply Chain

A key aspect of Green Ventures' strategy was the creation of a sustainable supply chain. This involved scrutinizing every step of the process, from raw material extraction to product delivery. Through partnerships with like-minded suppliers and the implementation of rigorous sustainability standards, Green Ventures ensured that its products were ethically sourced and environmentally friendly. This chapter highlights the critical role supply chain management plays in achieving true sustainability.

The journey to build a green supply chain began with a comprehensive assessment of the company's existing suppliers and their environmental practices. Green Ventures developed a set of sustainability criteria that suppliers were required to meet, including the use of renewable resources, waste reduction, and fair labor practices. This chapter explores the collaborative efforts between Green Ventures and its suppliers to achieve these standards and the positive outcomes that resulted.

One of the innovative approaches Green Ventures employed in its supply chain was the use of blockchain technology to enhance transparency and traceability. This chapter delves into how blockchain was used to track the origin and journey of raw materials, ensuring that they were sourced ethically and sustainably. The implementation of blockchain not only improved supply chain efficiency but also built trust with consumers by providing verifiable information about the sustainability of products.

The chapter concludes by discussing the broader impact of Green Ventures' green supply chain on the industry and the environment. By setting high sustainability standards and demonstrating their feasibility, Green Ventures encouraged other companies to adopt similar practices. The company's green supply chain also contributed to the reduction of environmental impacts associated with production and distribution, supporting global efforts to address climate change and promote sustainable development.

5

Chapter 5: Innovating with Green Technology

Innovation was at the heart of Green Ventures' operations. The company invested heavily in research and development to pioneer green technologies that would revolutionize its industry. This chapter explores the cutting-edge advancements in green technology spearheaded by Green Ventures, from biodegradable materials to energy-efficient manufacturing processes. It also examines the impact these innovations had on the market and the broader community.

Green Ventures recognized the potential of green technology to drive sustainable growth and address environmental challenges. This chapter delves into the company's efforts to develop and deploy innovative solutions, such as biodegradable packaging materials that reduced plastic waste and energy-efficient manufacturing processes that minimized carbon emissions. The company's commitment to continuous improvement and experimentation fostered a culture of creativity and progress.

One of the standout achievements of Green Ventures in the realm of green technology was the development of a closed-loop production system. This system aimed to eliminate waste by recycling and reusing materials throughout the production process. This chapter examines the technical intricacies of the closed-loop system, highlighting the engineering breakthroughs and collaborative efforts that made it possible. The system not only reduced environmental impact but also improved operational efficiency and cost-effectiveness.

The chapter concludes by discussing the broader implications of Green Ventures' green technology initiatives. By setting new standards for innovation and sustainability, the company inspired other businesses to invest in green technology and pursue similar advancements. Green Ventures' success demonstrated that environmental responsibility and technological progress could go hand in hand, paving the way for a more sustainable and prosperous future.

6

Chapter 6: Community Engagement and Corporate Social Responsibility

Green Ventures understood that true sustainability extends beyond the confines of the business. This chapter delves into the company's initiatives to engage with the community and foster a culture of environmental responsibility. From educational programs in local schools to collaborative projects with non-profit organizations, Green Ventures' efforts to give back to the community were both impactful and inspiring.

Community engagement was a core value of Green Ventures, rooted in the belief that businesses have a responsibility to contribute positively to society. This chapter explores the various programs and initiatives the company implemented to support and uplift local communities. These included environmental education programs in schools, tree-planting campaigns, and partnerships with non-profits to address pressing social and environmental issues.

One of the key components of Green Ventures' corporate social responsibility (CSR) strategy was employee volunteerism. The company encouraged its employees to actively participate in community service projects, providing paid time off and resources to support their efforts. This chapter highlights the positive outcomes of employee volunteerism, both for the community and for the company's culture. By fostering a sense of purpose and community among its employees, Green Ventures strengthened its commitment to social and environmental stewardship.

The chapter concludes by reflecting on the broader impact of Green Ventures' community engagement and CSR efforts. By prioritizing social responsibility and investing in the well-being of the community, the company built strong relationships and trust with stakeholders. Green Ventures' holistic approach to sustainability demonstrated that businesses could be powerful agents of positive change, creating a ripple effect that extended far beyond their immediate operations.

7

Chapter 7: Navigating Regulatory Landscapes

Operating sustainably often means navigating complex regulatory landscapes. This chapter explores the legal and regulatory challenges Green Ventures faced and how it successfully advocated for progressive policies. Through strategic lobbying and collaboration with government agencies, Green Ventures not only complied with existing regulations but also influenced the creation of new laws that promoted sustainability.

Green Ventures' commitment to sustainability required a proactive approach to regulatory compliance. This chapter examines the company's efforts to stay ahead of evolving environmental regulations and ensure that its operations met the highest standards of environmental protection. This involved working closely with legal experts and industry associations to understand and address regulatory requirements.

One of the significant challenges Green Ventures encountered was the variability of environmental regulations across different regions and countries. This chapter delves into the strategies the company employed to navigate these complexities, including the establishment of dedicated compliance teams and the development of standardized practices that could be adapted to different regulatory environments. The company's ability to harmonize its operations with diverse regulations was a testament to its resilience and adaptability.

The chapter concludes by discussing Green Ventures' role in shaping environmental policy. By advocating for progressive regulations and participating in policy-making processes, the company influenced the creation of laws that supported sustainable business practices. Green Ventures' efforts to engage with policymakers and promote sustainability at the legislative level underscored its commitment to driving systemic change and fostering a more sustainable future.

8

Chapter 8: Ethical Marketing and Consumer Trust

Marketing played a pivotal role in Green Ventures' strategy to build consumer trust and brand loyalty. This chapter examines how the company leveraged ethical marketing practices to resonate with environmentally conscious consumers. By maintaining transparency and authenticity in its messaging, Green Ventures was able to cultivate a loyal customer base that shared its values.

Green Ventures understood that ethical marketing was essential to building a strong and credible brand. This chapter explores the company's approach to marketing, which prioritized honesty, transparency, and authenticity. By providing clear and accurate information about its products and sustainability practices, Green Ventures established trust with consumers and differentiated itself from competitors.

One of the key elements of Green Ventures' ethical marketing strategy was the use of certifications and labels to validate its sustainability claims. This chapter delves into the various certifications the company obtained, such as Fair Trade, Organic, and Carbon Neutral, and how these labels reinforced the company's commitment to ethical practices. The chapter also examines the role of storytelling in Green Ventures' marketing efforts, highlighting how the company used narratives to connect with consumers on an emotional level and inspire positive action.

The chapter concludes by discussing the broader impact of Green Ventures' ethical marketing on the industry and consumer behavior. By setting an example of transparency and integrity, the company encouraged other businesses to adopt similar practices. Green Ventures' success demonstrated that ethical marketing could be a powerful tool for building brand loyalty and driving consumer engagement, ultimately contributing to a more sustainable and ethical marketplace.

9

Chapter 9: Overcoming Industry Resistance

Not everyone was on board with Green Ventures' mission. This chapter recounts the resistance the company faced from traditional industry players who were reluctant to adopt sustainable practices. Through perseverance and strategic alliances, Green Ventures was able to overcome these obstacles and demonstrate the viability of its business model.

The journey to sustainability was met with skepticism and opposition from established industry giants. This chapter explores the various forms of resistance Green Ventures encountered, from dismissive attitudes to active efforts to undermine the company's initiatives. Despite these challenges, Green Ventures remained steadfast in its commitment to sustainability and leveraged its innovative approach to differentiate itself in the market.

One of the key strategies Green Ventures employed to overcome industry resistance was building strategic alliances with like-minded organizations and thought leaders. This chapter delves into the collaborative efforts that helped amplify Green Ventures' message and garner support from influential stakeholders. By forming partnerships with environmental NGOs, academic institutions, and forward-thinking businesses, Green Ventures created a robust network of advocates for sustainable practices.

The chapter concludes by reflecting on the broader impact of Green Ventures' perseverance. By standing firm in the face of resistance, the company not only achieved its sustainability goals but also influenced the industry to re-evaluate its practices. Green Ventures' success demonstrated that sustainable business models were not only viable but also essential for long-term growth and resilience. The company's journey serves as an inspiring example of how determination and collaboration can drive meaningful change in the face of adversity.

10

Chapter 10: The Power of Collaboration

Collaboration was a key component of Green Ventures' success. This chapter explores the various partnerships and alliances the company formed with other businesses, non-profits, and government entities. By working together towards a common goal, Green Ventures was able to amplify its impact and drive broader industry change.

Green Ventures recognized that achieving sustainability required collective effort. This chapter delves into the company's collaborative approach, highlighting key partnerships that played a pivotal role in advancing its mission. From joint ventures with other sustainable businesses to collaborative research projects with universities, Green Ventures leveraged the power of collaboration to innovate and scale its impact.

One of the standout collaborations in Green Ventures' journey was its partnership with government agencies to promote green policies and initiatives. This chapter examines how the company worked with policymakers to advocate for supportive regulations and incentives for sustainable practices. The collaborative efforts led to the development of programs that encouraged businesses to adopt environmentally friendly operations and contributed to the broader goal of creating a sustainable economy.

The chapter concludes by discussing the broader implications of Green Ventures' collaborative approach. By fostering a culture of cooperation and shared purpose, the company was able to drive systemic change and influence industry standards. Green Ventures' success underscores the importance of collaboration in addressing global sustainability challenges and highlights the potential for collective action to create a more sustainable and equitable future.

11

Chapter 11: Measuring Impact and Sustainability Metrics

To ensure accountability and continuous improvement, Green Ventures implemented robust sustainability metrics. This chapter delves into the tools and methodologies the company used to measure its environmental and social impact. It also highlights the importance of transparency and how Green Ventures communicated its progress to stakeholders.

Green Ventures understood that meaningful sustainability efforts required accurate measurement and reporting. This chapter explores the company's approach to developing and implementing sustainability metrics, which encompassed a wide range of indicators, including carbon footprint, water usage, waste generation, and social impact. By adopting a data-driven approach, Green Ventures was able to track its progress and identify areas for improvement.

One of the innovative tools used by Green Ventures was the integration of environmental, social, and governance (ESG) criteria into its performance evaluation. This chapter delves into how the company used ESG metrics to assess its overall impact and align its operations with sustainability goals. The chapter also examines the role of third-party audits and certifications in enhancing the credibility and transparency of Green Ventures' sustainability reporting.

The chapter concludes by discussing the importance of communication and stakeholder engagement in the context of sustainability metrics. Green Ventures prioritized transparency by regularly publishing sustainability reports and engaging with stakeholders through various channels. By sharing its achievements and challenges openly, the company built trust and accountability with its stakeholders and inspired other businesses to adopt similar practices.

12

Chapter 12: Navigating Financial Challenges

Sustainability often comes with financial challenges. This chapter explores the economic obstacles Green Ventures encountered and the creative solutions it devised to maintain financial stability. From securing funding to managing operational costs, the company's financial strategies were a testament to its resilience and ingenuity.

Green Ventures faced significant financial challenges, particularly in the early stages of its journey. This chapter delves into the various economic hurdles the company encountered, including the higher upfront costs of sustainable materials and technologies. Despite these challenges, Green Ventures remained committed to its sustainability goals and sought innovative solutions to overcome financial constraints.

One of the key strategies employed by Green Ventures was securing funding from impact investors and green investment funds. This chapter explores how the company attracted investors who shared its vision for sustainability and were willing to support its long-term goals. The chapter also examines the role of government grants and incentives in alleviating financial pressures and enabling Green Ventures to invest in sustainable initiatives.

The chapter concludes by highlighting Green Ventures' approach to cost management and operational efficiency. By implementing lean manufacturing practices and optimizing resource utilization, the company was able to reduce operational costs and improve financial performance. Green Ventures' ability to navigate financial challenges demonstrated its resilience and adaptability, setting an example for other businesses striving to balance sustainability and profitability.

13

Chapter 13: Scaling Sustainable Practices Globally

With success at home, Green Ventures aimed to expand its reach globally. This chapter chronicles the company's efforts to scale its sustainable practices to international markets. It examines the cultural, logistical, and regulatory challenges of operating in diverse regions and how Green Ventures adapted its strategies to thrive globally.

Green Ventures' vision extended beyond national borders, as the company sought to make a global impact. This chapter explores the company's international expansion strategy, which involved identifying key markets, establishing local partnerships, and adapting its practices to meet regional needs and regulations. The chapter highlights the importance of cultural sensitivity and local engagement in successfully scaling sustainable practices.

One of the significant challenges Green Ventures faced in its global expansion was navigating different regulatory environments. This chapter delves into the strategies the company employed to ensure compliance with diverse environmental regulations and standards. By working closely with local authorities and leveraging its expertise in sustainability, Green Ventures was able to overcome regulatory hurdles and establish a strong presence in international markets.

The chapter concludes by discussing the broader impact of Green Ventures' global expansion. By bringing its sustainable practices to new regions, the company contributed to the global sustainability movement and inspired other businesses to follow suit. Green Ventures' success in scaling its operations globally demonstrated the potential for sustainable businesses to drive positive change on a worldwide scale.

14

Chapter 14: Inspiring the Next Generation

Green Ventures believed in the power of education to drive long-term change. This chapter focuses on the company's initiatives to inspire and empower the next generation of environmental stewards. Through mentorship programs, scholarships, and partnerships with educational institutions, Green Ventures planted the seeds of sustainability in the minds of young leaders.

Education was a cornerstone of Green Ventures' mission to create a sustainable future. This chapter explores the various educational programs and initiatives the company developed to promote environmental awareness and sustainability. These included school outreach programs, where Green Ventures' employees volunteered to teach students about the importance of protecting the environment and the role of sustainable practices in achieving this goal.

One of the key components of Green Ventures' educational efforts was the establishment of scholarships and mentorship programs for students pursuing careers in sustainability-related fields. This chapter delves into the impact of these programs, highlighting the stories of students who benefited from Green Ventures' support and went on to become influential advocates for sustainability. The company's investment in education not only empowered individual students but also contributed to the broader goal of building a more environmentally conscious society.

The chapter concludes by discussing the importance of collaboration with educational institutions. Green Ventures formed partnerships with universities and research centers to advance sustainability research and innovation. By supporting academic research and providing practical learning opportunities for students, the company fostered a new generation of leaders equipped with the knowledge and skills to address global environmental challenges. The chapter underscores the enduring legacy of Green Ventures' commitment to education and its role in shaping a sustainable future.

15

Chapter 15: The Future of Green Ventures

As the book draws to a close, this final chapter reflects on the journey of Green Ventures and envisions its future. It explores the company's long-term goals, emerging trends in sustainability, and the potential challenges that lie ahead. The chapter concludes with a call to action, encouraging readers to join Green Ventures in pioneering a more sustainable and ethical global arena.

Green Ventures' journey was marked by significant achievements and milestones, but the company's vision for the future remained ambitious. This chapter delves into the long-term goals of Green Ventures, which included expanding its global reach, continuing to innovate with green technologies, and advocating for progressive environmental policies. The company's commitment to continuous improvement and adaptation positioned it as a leader in the sustainability movement.

One of the emerging trends in sustainability that Green Ventures embraced was the circular economy. This chapter explores the company's efforts to transition from a linear economy, characterized by a take-make-dispose model, to a circular economy that emphasizes the reuse, recycling, and regeneration of materials. By adopting circular economy principles, Green Ventures aimed to minimize waste and create a more sustainable and resilient business model.

The chapter also examines the potential challenges Green Ventures faced in its pursuit of sustainability. These included evolving regulatory landscapes, economic uncertainties, and the need for continuous innovation. Despite these challenges, Green Ventures remained optimistic and committed to its mission. The company's resilience and adaptability were key factors in its ability to navigate a complex and ever-changing global environment.

The book concludes with a call to action, encouraging readers to join Green Ventures in its mission to pioneer sustainability and ethical practices in the global arena. By highlighting the collective effort required to address global environmental challenges, the chapter underscores the importance of individual and collective action. Green Ventures' story serves as an inspiring example of how businesses can be powerful agents of positive change, and the book invites readers to be part of this transformative journey.

Book Description: Green Ventures: Pioneering Sustainability and Ethical Practices in the Global Arena

"Green Ventures: Pioneering Sustainability and Ethical Practices in the Global Arena" takes readers on an inspiring journey through the evolution of a visionary company dedicated to reshaping the business landscape with sustainable and ethical practices. Founded by the passionate entrepreneur Lila Patel, Green Ventures emerges as a beacon of hope amid the challenges of industrialization and environmental degradation.

This book delves into the heart of Green Ventures' mission, illustrating how the company integrated eco-economics, harnessed renewable resources, and built a green supply chain. Each chapter vividly portrays the company's innovative approach to overcoming industry resistance, navigating regulatory landscapes, and leveraging ethical marketing to earn consumer trust.

Readers will be captivated by the accounts of Green Ventures' cutting-edge technological advancements, community engagement initiatives, and the power of collaboration that propelled the company to global prominence. The book also highlights the importance of measuring impact and navigating financial challenges while scaling sustainable practices internationally.

As the narrative unfolds, it becomes clear that Green Ventures' legacy extends far beyond its products and operations. The company's commitment to education and inspiring the next generation of environmental stewards

CHAPTER 15: THE FUTURE OF GREEN VENTURES

underscores its dedication to a sustainable future. The concluding chapters envision the future of Green Ventures and call readers to join in the mission of pioneering sustainability and ethical practices on a global scale.

"Green Ventures: Pioneering Sustainability and Ethical Practices in the Global Arena" is a testament to the power of vision, innovation, and collective action. It serves as a powerful reminder that businesses can be agents of positive change, creating a better world for future generations. Whether you are a business leader, an environmental advocate, or simply someone who cares about the planet, this book will inspire and empower you to make a difference.

www.ingramcontent.com/pod-product-compliance
Lightning Source LLC
LaVergne TN
LVHW020502080526
838202LV00057B/6102